Echoes of the Gayatri

The Power of Sacred Chant

SAIRAM ABBIREDDY

Contents

Acknowledgments

I extend my deepest gratitude to my parents, whose unwavering love and support have been the foundation of my journey. Their guidance and belief in the power of prayer have inspired every word of this book. To my teachers, thank you for imparting wisdom and nurturing my spiritual curiosity, guiding me toward understanding the deeper meaning of life. My heartfelt appreciation also goes to my friends, who have been a source of encouragement and inspiration throughout this writing process. *"Echoes of the Gayatri: The Power of Sacred Chant"* is a reflection of all your contributions and blessings.

Introduction

In today's fast-moving world, the search for inner peace and spiritual connection has never been more important. *Echoes of the Gayatri: The Power of Sacred Chant* takes you on a journey into the heart of prayer - its many forms, its transformative energy, and its ability to bring solace, clarity, and strength.

Prayer is more than just a ritual; it is a bridge between the ordinary and the divine. Whether it is a quiet moment of meditation or a heartfelt spoken invocation, every form of prayer nurtures the soul and deepens our spiritual essence.

At the core of this exploration lies the **Gayatri Mantra** - an ancient and revered chant that has resonated through time. More than just words, this sacred mantra carries a powerful vibrational energy that aligns us with the universe's rhythms, opening the door to higher consciousness and enlightenment.

In *Echoes of the Gayatri*, we will uncover the essence of prayer and the profound impact of the **Gayatri Mantra**. Through this journey, you will discover how these timeless practices can enrich your life by bringing peace, clarity, and a deeper connection with the divine.

1: What is Prayer?

Prayer is a practice that transcends cultures, religions, and spiritual beliefs, forming a fundamental part of human existence. At its core, prayer is a deliberate and heartfelt communication with a higher power, the divine, or a spiritual presence. It is more than just words - it is an act of reaching beyond oneself, seeking **connection, guidance, and comfort**.

Personal Reflection

I still remember the first time I truly engaged in prayer. As a child, I would recite simple prayers before meals and bedtime with my family. At that time, I didn't fully understand the depth of what I was doing, it was just a routine. But as I grew older, my perspective changed. I began to see prayer not as a mere ritual but as a **powerful practice** - a sacred conversation with the divine, filled with meaning and intention.

Types of Prayer

Prayer can take many forms, each serving a unique purpose. While countless variations exist, these six types of prayer are among the most commonly practiced:

1. Petition - Asking for Divine Help

Petitionary prayer is when we ask for something - help, guidance, or intervention. It is the most common form of prayer, as it comes naturally in moments of uncertainty or need.

For instance, Mahalakshmi, a woman facing a difficult career decision, turned to prayer for clarity. She prayed, not just for an answer, but for **wisdom to make the right choice**. Over time, she found herself more in tune with her values and aspirations, ultimately making a decision that aligned with her true calling.

2. Intercession – Praying for Others

Intercessory prayer is when we pray on behalf of someone else. It is an act of compassion and selflessness, asking for divine assistance for others.

Imagine a community coming together to pray for a loved one who is ill. Their prayers form a circle of support, offering not only spiritual strength but also emotional comfort. In many traditions, intercessory prayer is seen as a way to uplift and heal.

3. Thanksgiving – Expressing Gratitude

Thanksgiving prayer is about **gratitude**, acknowledging the blessings and good things in life. This form of prayer fosters contentment and positivity.

I recall moments when I felt overwhelmed by challenges, yet taking time to offer a prayer of gratitude shifted my perspective. Instead of focusing on what was missing, I learned to appreciate the good already present in my life. Gratitude through prayer can be a powerful way to develop an abundant and joyful mindset.

4. Praise – Honoring the Divine

Praise prayer is all about adoration and reverence. It is an expression of love and appreciation for the divine, celebrating its presence, power, and goodness.

Many religious traditions incorporate praise through hymns, songs, or spoken words. Whether in a temple, church, or personal space, engaging in praise prayer can be a deeply moving experience, filling the heart with a sense of divine closeness.

5. Confession – Seeking Forgiveness and Renewal

Confession prayer is about acknowledging mistakes, regrets, and shortcomings. It is an honest moment of self-reflection, asking for divine mercy and the strength to move forward.

During a difficult time in my life, I turned to confession prayer, admitting my faults, and seeking inner healing. The act of surrendering my burdens through prayer helped me experience a deep sense of release and renewal, allowing me to grow from my past.

6. Meditation – Listening in Silence

Meditative prayer is not about speaking but listening. It is a reflective practice that helps cultivate inner peace and deeper awareness.

Different spiritual traditions incorporate meditation, whether through silent contemplation, mantra repetition, or sacred texts. Personally, engaging in meditation has brought moments of deep serenity and connection with the divine, reminding me that prayer is as much about listening as it is about speaking.

2: The Power of Prayer

Prayer has a quiet yet profound power - it transforms, heals, and uplifts. It isn't just about asking for something; it's about deepening our connection with ourselves, with others, and with the divine. Whether whispered in solitude or spoken in a gathering, prayer can shape our thoughts, emotions, and even our circumstances in ways that go beyond explanation.

1. Personal Transformation

One of the most beautiful aspects of prayer is how it changes the person who prays. It's not just about finding answers, it's about finding ourselves. Through prayer, we gain clarity, emotional strength, and a sense of purpose. It teaches us to pause, reflect, and listen to that inner voice guiding us forward.

Looking back, I realize how much prayer has shaped my own journey. There were moments of doubt, of feeling lost, yet prayer became my anchor. It didn't always provide immediate answers, but it gave me the strength to navigate through life's uncertainties with faith and resilience.

2. Emotional Support

Life is filled with moments of joy, but also with hardships. In times of loss, fear, or confusion, prayer becomes a refuge - a place where we can pour out our emotions without judgment, where we can find comfort in the presence of something greater than ourselves.

I remember a time when grief weighed heavily on me, making every day feel like an uphill battle. During those days, prayer was my solace. Even though it didn't take away the pain, it gave me the strength to endure, to heal, and to move forward with a heart that still carried love.

3. Strengthening Relationships

Prayer isn't just a personal experience; it can also bring people together. Whether it's a family praying before a meal, a group coming together in faith, or simply a friend offering a silent prayer for another, these moments create bonds that go beyond words.

Some of my most cherished memories are of praying with loved ones, times when faith brought us closer, when shared prayers created an unspoken understanding between us. Prayer has a way of reminding us that we're not alone, that we have each other to lean on.

4. Influencing Outcomes

Prayer isn't about miracles alone, but sometimes, it feels like one. Whether it's divine intervention or the power of focused belief, there's something about sincere prayer that seems to shift circumstances in unexpected ways.

I've experienced this firsthand. Before my ecology exam, I was unwell and barely had time to study. I felt overwhelmed, convinced that I would fail. Yet, in those moments of fear, I turned to prayer. I asked for strength, for clarity and somehow, despite all odds, I not only passed but scored the highest marks in that subject. Was it faith? Was it focus? Maybe both. But that experience showed me the incredible ways prayer can work in our lives.

5. Fostering Gratitude and Positivity

One of the simplest yet most profound aspects of prayer is how it shifts our focus from what we lack to what we have. It teaches us to pause and recognize the blessings in our lives, no matter how small.

Taking a moment each day to offer a prayer of gratitude has changed my perspective. Instead of dwelling on what's missing, I find myself appreciating the warmth of the sun, the kindness of a friend, the gift of another day. Prayer doesn't erase challenges, but it helps us face them with a heart full of gratitude.

3: Developing a Prayer Life

Setting Aside Dedicated Prayer Time

Creating a habit of prayer is much like building any meaningful routine - it requires intention, consistency, and a bit of patience. Just as we nourish our bodies with food and rest, our spiritual selves also need regular moments of connection and reflection. Setting aside a dedicated time for prayer helps bring structure to this practice, allowing us to deepen our faith and cultivate a sense of inner peace.

Psychological and neurological research supports the idea that structured routines, including prayer, contribute to overall wellbeing. Regular spiritual engagement has been linked to lower stress levels, improved emotional resilience, and even enhanced cognitive function. Having a specific time for prayer can offer stability, a moment of stillness amidst life's constant movement.

I've noticed that when I commit to a specific prayer time, whether it's early in the morning before the day begins or in the quiet of the evening, it transforms the experience. It becomes more than a habit; it turns into a moment of solace, clarity, and renewed strength. Some days, it feels like a deep conversation; other days, it's simply a silent acknowledgment of gratitude. But in all cases, it grounds me.

Finding a Quiet Place to Pray

Where we pray can make a difference in how we experience it. A peaceful, distraction-free space allows us to quiet our minds and open our hearts more fully. It doesn't have to be elaborate: a simple corner in a room, a spot in a park, or even a seat by a window can become a sacred space. The key is finding a place where we feel comfortable, undisturbed, and connected.

Studies show that being in quiet environments, especially those close to nature, can lower stress levels and enhance our mood. This aligns with what many spiritual traditions have known for centuries: a calm setting encourages deeper reflection and a greater sense of presence.

I've found that having a dedicated prayer space changes my experience significantly. Whether it's a cozy nook with a candle or a serene outdoor spot where the breeze carries my thoughts, the atmosphere shapes the depth of my prayer. When I step into that space, it's like my soul recognizes it's time to slow down and connect.

Incorporating Prayer into Daily Activities

While setting aside specific prayer time is important, integrating prayer into daily life can create a continuous sense of connection with the divine. Prayer doesn't always have to be a structured event: it can flow naturally into the rhythm of our day. A silent blessing before a meal, a moment of gratitude while taking a walk, or even a whispered prayer during a challenging moment can infuse the ordinary with a sense of the sacred.

This practice closely mirrors the concept of mindfulness, where being present in the moment enhances emotional well-being and reduces stress. Studies suggest that mindfulness-based practices, including spiritual reflection, help with emotional regulation and overall mental health. By incorporating prayer into everyday moments like during a morning routine, while cooking, or even amid a busy commute - we can foster a deeper awareness of the divine in all aspects of life.

For me, some of my most meaningful prayers have happened in unexpected moments - watching the sunrise, sipping tea in the quiet of the morning, or even just taking a deep breath before a big decision. These little acts of connection remind me that prayer isn't just about setting time aside - it's about carrying that sense of presence and awareness throughout the day.

4: The "*Gayatri Mantra*" and Its Transformative Power

The **Gayatri Mantra** is one of the most revered hymns in Hindu spirituality, carrying deep significance across generations. Found in the *Rigveda*, one of the world's oldest sacred texts, this mantra is dedicated to *Savitr*, the Sun deity, and is considered a source of spiritual illumination and divine wisdom. Those who chant it with sincerity often describe experiencing profound inner peace, clarity, and transformation.

The Gayatri Mantra

Traditionally recited in Sanskrit, the Gayatri Mantra is as follows:

"Om Bhur Bhuvah Svah

Tat Savitur Varenyam

Bhargo Devasya Dhimahi

Dhiyo Yo Nah Prachodayat." A simple translation of this powerful verse:

"Om, we meditate on the divine essence that pervades the Earth, Atmosphere, and Heaven. May the supreme divine light of Savitr inspire and illuminate our intellects."

The Meaning and Spiritual Power

Every word in the **Gayatri Mantra** holds deep spiritual significance:

"Om" - The universal sound, representing the essence of the divine.

"Bhur, Bhuvah, Svah" - These words symbolize the three realms: Earth (physical world), Atmosphere (mental world), and Heaven (spiritual realm).

"Tat Savitur Varenyam" - Acknowledges Savitr, the divine Sun, the ultimate source of light and wisdom.

"Bhargo Devasya Dhimahi" - A meditation on the divine radiance that purifies and uplifts.

"Dhiyo Yo Nah Prachodayat" - A heartfelt prayer asking for divine guidance and enlightenment.

How the Gayatri Mantra Transforms Lives

Beyond its spiritual significance, the **Gayatri Mantra** has been associated with a wide range of mental, emotional, and physical benefits. Modern research on sound vibrations and meditation has also echoed these benefits, suggesting that regular chanting can positively influence our overall well-being.

1. Enhancing Mental Clarity and Focus

The rhythmic repetition of the mantra has a calming effect on the mind, reducing distractions and sharpening concentration. Many students and professionals use it to clear their thoughts and improve decision-making. Studies on sound vibrations suggest that chanting certain frequencies can enhance cognitive function and improve attention spans.

2. Reducing Stress and Cultivating Emotional Stability

In today's fast-paced world, stress is a common challenge. Chanting the Gayatri Mantra activates the parasympathetic nervous system, helping to lower stress hormones like cortisol. This creates a natural relaxation response, reducing anxiety and promoting emotional balance. Many practitioners describe feeling a deep sense of calm after even a few minutes of recitation.

3. Awakening Spiritual Awareness

More than just words, the Gayatri Mantra carries an energy that aligns the practitioner with higher spiritual vibrations. Regular recitation can lead to increased self-awareness, mindfulness, and a deeper connection with the divine. It becomes a tool for introspection, helping individuals navigate life with greater wisdom and inner peace.

4. Boosting Physical Health and Vitality

There is growing evidence that spiritual practices, including mantra chanting, contribute to overall well-being. The vibrations created by chanting the Gayatri Mantra can help balance the body's energy systems, improve respiratory function, and even enhance immunity. Many devotees believe that the mantra acts as a purifier, harmonizing both the body and mind.

Real-Life Transformations

The Gayatri Mantra has left a profound impact on countless lives. Many practitioners share how it has helped them overcome **moments of doubt, fear, or confusion**, guiding them toward clarity and strength. Some describe its ability to provide **mental peace during times of emotional turmoil**, while others credit it for helping them make **better life decisions** with a clear and focused mind.

Whether one seeks wisdom, healing, or simply a moment of stillness in a chaotic world, the **Gayatri Mantra** serves as a guiding light. It is more than just a sacred chant: it is a bridge to the divine, a source of resilience, and a key to unlocking the highest potential within ourselves.

Chapter 5: Obstacles to Prayer

Prayer is meant to be a source of comfort, connection, and strength. But let's be honest - there are times when it feels anything but that. Sometimes, distractions take over. Other times, it feels like our prayers go unheard. And then there are moments when we wonder if we're even *worthy* of praying at all.

These struggles are real, and they can make prayer feel frustrating or even distant. But just because we face obstacles doesn't mean we should give up. Instead, by recognizing these challenges and learning how to navigate them, we can deepen our spiritual practice and strengthen our relationship with the divine.

Let's explore some of the common struggles we face in prayer and how we can overcome them.

Distractions: The Battle for Focus

One of the biggest struggles in prayer is simply *staying focused*. We live in a world full of distractions - phones buzzing, to-do lists piling up, and thoughts racing through our minds. Even when we sit down to pray, it's easy to get lost in a stream of unrelated thoughts.

I've been there. I've caught myself going through the motions of prayer while mentally planning my next day or worrying about an unfinished task. And before I knew it, my prayer felt rushed and disconnected.

How to Regain Focus in Prayer:

Create a Prayer Space – Find a quiet, dedicated space where you can pray without interruptions. It doesn't have to be elaborate; even a simple corner with a candle or sacred object can set the right tone.

Set a Prayer Routine – Just like any habit, prayer becomes more natural when it's part of a routine. Setting a specific time each day morning, night, or even during a lunch break can help.

Use Mindfulness Techniques – If your mind tends to wander, try focusing on your breath or repeating a short phrase (like a mantra or a line from a prayer). This can help anchor your thoughts.

When Prayers Seem Unanswered

One of the hardest things to grapple with is when prayers go unanswered. We pour our hearts out, ask for guidance, hope for a change… and nothing seems to happen. It can feel disheartening, even like we've been forgotten.

I remember a time when I prayed endlessly for something I deeply wanted. When things didn't work out the way I had hoped, I felt lost. I wondered if my prayers even mattered. But over time, I realized that sometimes, the answers come in ways we don't expect or in ways we can only understand later.

How to Find Peace with Unanswered Prayers:

Shift Your Perspective – Maybe what we're asking for isn't what's best for us in the long run. Sometimes, the divine has a bigger plan, one that we can't fully see yet.

Look for Growth – Unanswered prayers can teach us patience, resilience, and trust. They might push us toward paths we never considered but that turn out to be even better.

Seek Support – If you're struggling with disappointment in prayer, talk to someone you trust : a spiritual mentor, a close friend, or even a faith-based community. Their perspectives and encouragement can help you process your feelings.

Feeling Unworthy: The Inner Struggle

Have you ever felt like you don't deserve to pray? Maybe because of past mistakes, doubts, or a sense of guilt? If so, you're not alone. Many people struggle with the belief that they aren't "good enough" to approach the divine.

I've had moments where I questioned whether I was worthy of divine attention. I wondered if my flaws and failures made me undeserving. But prayer isn't about being *perfect* - it's about being *honest*.

How to Overcome Feelings of Unworthiness in Prayer:

Embrace Forgiveness – Many spiritual traditions teach that forgiveness is always available. Prayer isn't a privilege for the perfect - it's a refuge for those who seek healing and growth.

Remind Yourself of Your Worth – You are *always* worthy of love, grace, and connection. No mistake or shortcoming can change that.

See Prayer as a Journey, Not a Test – Prayer isn't about proving yourself. It's about growing, learning, and deepening your relationship with the divine one step at a time.

Moving Forward: Perseverance and Faith

Obstacles in prayer are natural, but they don't have to stop us. If we push through distractions, trust in the divine even when prayers go unanswered, and remind ourselves that we are always worthy, we can develop a stronger, more meaningful connection in prayer.

Here's how to keep going, even when it's hard:

Stay Consistent – Even if your prayers feel dry or distracted, keep showing up. Over time, consistency builds depth.

Be Open to Change – Prayer evolves as we grow. Let it be a dynamic, living practice rather than something rigid.

Find Inspiration – Read spiritual texts, listen to uplifting messages, or learn from those who inspire you. Sometimes, a fresh perspective can reignite your passion for prayer.

Chapter 6: Praying for Others

Praying for others is one of the most selfless acts of love and compassion. It's a way of reaching beyond ourselves, offering comfort, strength, and hope to those in need. Whether we are praying for a loved one's healing, for peace in the world, or simply sending positive energy to someone struggling, these prayers create a deep sense of connection both to the divine and to each other.

Throughout history, people from all faiths and traditions have turned to prayer as a source of support, believing that it can bring about healing, guidance, and even miracles. Some prayers, like the *Gayatri Mantra* and the *Hanuman Chalisa*, are revered for their ability to invoke divine blessings, protection, and transformation.

The Power of Intercessory Prayer

Intercessory prayer is when we pray on behalf of someone else whether it's a friend, a family member, or even someone we've never met. It's an act of pure empathy, where we set aside our own worries and focus on the needs of others.

I remember a time when a close friend of mine was going through a difficult phase in life. She was struggling with uncertainty, and though I couldn't change her situation, I prayed for her every day. I asked for her strength, clarity, and peace. Over time, she found the courage to navigate her challenges, and while I can't claim my prayers were the reason, I do believe they created a sense of support and encouragement that helped her along the way.

Intercessory prayer isn't just about asking for miracles - it's about sending out thoughts of love, protection, and healing. When entire communities pray together for someone in distress, the collective energy of those prayers can be profoundly comforting.

Praying for the Sick and Suffering

When someone we love is sick or in pain, we often feel helpless. But prayer gives us something meaningful to do - it allows us to express our care and offer hope, even when medical interventions have their limits.

Many spiritual traditions hold the belief that prayers, chants, or mantras can bring healing energy to the person in need. It's not just about physical recovery; it's about providing emotional and spiritual strength. Sometimes, just knowing that people are praying for them can bring comfort to someone who is struggling. I recall visiting a hospital where volunteers would come daily to pray for patients: whether or not they knew them personally. It was deeply moving to witness. There was something incredibly powerful in the way they offered their prayers, not expecting anything in return, just hoping to bring a little peace to those suffering.

Praying for World Peace and Justice

Beyond personal struggles, we often pray for a better world. Whether it's for the end of violence, justice for the oppressed, or harmony between nations, these prayers reflect a longing for peace and fairness.

One of the most beautiful prayers for peace is the Sanskrit verse:

"Samastha Lokaah Sukhino Bhavantu"

(May all the beings in all the worlds be happy and free.)

This prayer goes beyond individual concerns - it is a universal wish for kindness, unity, and balance. In times of crisis, when the world feels chaotic and divided, such prayers remind us that we are all connected and that our hopes for peace and justice can transcend borders.

Sacred Prayers for Protection and Strength

Some prayers hold a special place in people's hearts for their perceived ability to bring divine intervention. Among them, the *Gayatri Mantra* and the *Hanuman Chalisa* are known for their protective and uplifting energy.

The Gayatri Mantra: A Prayer for Wisdom and Guidance

The *Gayatri Mantra* is one of the oldest and most revered Vedic hymns. It is a call for divine illumination, asking for wisdom and clarity in life.

"Om Bhur Bhuvah Swaha, Tat Savitur Varenyam, Bhargo Devasya Dhīmahi, Dhiyo Yo Nah Prachodayāt.."

This mantra is often recited not just for personal enlightenment but for the well-being of others. I have known people who chant the *Gayatri Mantra* daily for their loved ones, believing that it brings light into their lives, dispelling negativity and fear.

There was a woman I once met who recited the *Gayatri Mantra* for her son every morning before he left for work. She believed it would guide him, protect him, and give him strength to face the challenges of the day. Her unwavering faith in the power of prayer was truly inspiring.

The Hanuman Chalisa: A Prayer for Strength and Protection

The *Hanuman Chalisa,* a devotional hymn dedicated to Lord Hanuman, is another powerful prayer known for its ability to instill courage and overcome obstacles. It is often recited by those facing difficulties, seeking protection, or wishing for resilience in tough times.

Many believe that reciting the *Hanuman Chalisa* creates a shield of divine protection. It is often chanted by people praying for the well-being of their loved ones, asking Hanuman's strength to help them through hardships.

I remember my grandmother softly reciting the *Hanuman Chalisa* whenever our family faced a tough situation. Even when we didn't fully understand its meaning as children, her faith in the prayer's strength was enough to make us feel safe and reassured.

Chapter 7: The Science Behind Chanting

Many believe that chanting mantras is purely a spiritual or religious practice, but science reveals that sound vibrations have profound effects on the mind and body. When we chant the Gayatri Mantra, we engage in a rhythmic process that influences brain waves, heart rate, and even cellular activity. Research suggests that chanting mantras can reduce stress, lower blood pressure, and improve focus. This is because repetitive sound patterns create a meditative state, leading to deep relaxation.

One of the key elements of the Gayatri Mantra is its resonance. Each syllable vibrates at a particular frequency, and these vibrations interact with our energy centers (chakras), balancing and harmonizing them. Even without understanding Sanskrit, the sound itself has the power to create a sense of peace. This is why people across cultures use repetitive prayers, affirmations, or chants as a form of meditation.

Chapter 8: The Role of Intention in Prayer

Prayer is often misunderstood as a request for divine intervention, but at its core, it is an act of intention. The words we say, the emotions we feel, and the beliefs we hold all shape the outcome of our prayers. Scientific studies on intention and consciousness show that our thoughts have measurable effects on the world around us.

When chanting the Gayatri Mantra, the intention is key. It is not just about repeating words but about focusing our mind and heart on enlightenment, wisdom, and positive transformation. When chanted with sincerity, it can shift our perspective, helping us navigate challenges with clarity and grace. This is why some people find their lives changing after adopting a regular prayer practice—it is not just the act of praying but the deep, heartfelt intention behind it.

The Science of Intention

Research in quantum physics and psychology suggests that focused intention can influence outcomes. Experiments on the placebo effect demonstrate that belief alone can trigger healing responses in the body. Similarly, chanting the Gayatri Mantra with deep conviction creates an inner shift that radiates outward, affecting our emotional, mental, and even physical well-being.

Aligning Intention with Action

Setting an intention before chanting is like tuning an instrument before playing. Before you begin your practice, take a deep breath and focus on your purpose whether it is clarity, healing, or peace.

This alignment amplifies the power of the mantra, making it a truly transformative experience.

Chapter 9: How to Build a Consistent Chanting Practice

Starting a new habit can be challenging, but creating a structured routine makes it easier. Here are some practical steps to incorporate the Gayatri Mantra into your daily life:

1. Choosing the Right Time

Early mornings or evenings are ideal, as they are quieter and more conducive to meditation. The Brahma Muhurta (pre-dawn) is considered the most spiritually powerful time for chanting.

2. Creating a Sacred Space

A calm, clean space enhances focus. It can be a small corner with a mat, candle, or image that inspires devotion. Keeping the environment peaceful allows for deeper immersion in the practice.

3. Beginning with Small Steps

Start with five repetitions and gradually increase to 108 chants over time. Even a few repetitions daily can create a profound shift.

4. Using a Mala (Prayer Beads)

A mala helps maintain focus and builds a meditative rhythm. Moving through each bead with a chant keeps distractions at bay.

5. Understanding the Meaning

Before chanting, take a moment to contemplate the mantra's significance. Reflecting on its meaning enhances spiritual connection and devotion.

6. Maintaining Consistency

The key to experiencing transformation is consistency. Even if you miss a day, return to your practice without guilt. Over time, it will become an integral part of your life.

Chapter 10: The Gayatri Mantra as a Source of Healing

The Gayatri Mantra is often regarded as a source of light, wisdom, and clarity, but it also serves as a powerful healing tool. Many ancient traditions believe that sound can restore balance in the body. In Ayurveda, mantras are prescribed to support physical and mental healing.

The Healing Power of Sound

Scientific studies show that chanting reduces cortisol levels, which helps combat stress-related illnesses. The vibrations created by the mantra stimulate the vagus nerve, responsible for relaxation and emotional regulation. This is why people often experience a sense of relief, calmness, and even physical healing after a deep chanting session. **Clearing Negative Energy**

The mantra is known to clear negative energy and elevate consciousness, helping individuals let go of past trauma, anxiety, and emotional blocks. It acts as a guiding light, reminding us that we are not alone but connected to a greater universal force.

Chapter 11: Overcoming Doubts and Skepticism

In the modern world, skepticism about spiritual practices is common. Many wonder: How can a simple chant affect my life? The answer lies in experience. The true power of the Gayatri Mantra is not in reading about it but in practicing it.

Facing Inner Doubts

Doubt is natural, especially when approaching spiritual practices with a scientific mindset. However, even great scientists like Nikola Tesla and Albert Einstein acknowledged the presence of higher frequencies and energy fields beyond ordinary perception.

A 40-Day Experiment

If you have doubts, start with an open mind. Try chanting the mantra consistently for 40 days and observe the changes in your thoughts, emotions, and interactions with the world. Spirituality is deeply personal, and no one else can convince you of its benefits only experience can.

Chapter 12: The Power of Group Chanting

Chanting in solitude is deeply transformative, but chanting in a group amplifies its energy. When voices merge in unison, they create a collective vibrational field that is far more potent than an individual effort. Many spiritual traditions encourage group chanting for this reason.

Scientific research suggests that synchronized chanting can harmonize brainwave activity, creating a profound sense of unity and peace. Communities that engage in collective prayer often report higher levels of emotional resilience and mental clarity.

If you ever have the chance to chant the Gayatri Mantra in a group setting be it in a temple, an online gathering, or with friends embrace the experience. You may find it even more powerful than your solo practice.

Chapter 13: A Final Reflection - The Power of Collective Prayer

The Gayatri Mantra is more than just a set of words—it is a living, breathing experience of transformation. It has the power to elevate consciousness, provide clarity, and bring inner peace.

Through this book, I hope you have found inspiration to embrace prayer and chanting as a meaningful part of your life.

A profound experience in my own life reinforced my faith in the divine power of prayer. A close friend's father met with a terrible accident, and doctors feared he would require major surgery. Worried and feeling helpless, we, a group of friends in our hostel, came together and chanted the Maha Mrityunjaya Mantra –
Tryambakam Yajamahe Sugandhim Pushtivardhanam, Urvarukamiva Bandhanan Mrityor Mukshiya Maamritat. With all our hearts, we prayed for his well-being. Miraculously, by the divine's grace, his condition improved overnight, and he escaped the surgery. This experience deepened my conviction that prayer when done with sincerity and collective devotion, has the power to bring about healing and protection.

Remember that the light within you is always shining no matter where you are on your spiritual journey. All you need to do is recognize, nurture, and let it guide you toward a life of wisdom, love, and fulfillment.

Chapter 14: The Synergy Between the Gayatri Mantra and the Maha Mrityunjaya Mantra

The Gayatri Mantra and the Maha Mrityunjaya Mantra uniquely complement each other. While the Gayatri Mantra brings wisdom, clarity, and spiritual illumination, the Maha Mrityunjaya Mantra provides protection, health, and resilience.

Some practitioners incorporate both into their daily practice:

- **Morning Chanting:** Start the day with the Gayatri Mantra to invoke divine wisdom and mental clarity.

- **Evening Chanting:** End the day with the Maha Mrityunjaya Mantra to seek protection and healing from the challenges faced during the day.

This balance between enlightenment and protection creates harmony in life, fostering both spiritual growth and worldly wellbeing.

Conclusion

As I bring *Echoes of the Gayatri: The Power of Sacred Chant* to a close, I find myself reflecting on the journey that led me to write this book. Prayer has been more than just a practice for me, it has been a guiding light, a source of comfort, and a wellspring of strength during life's challenges. Among all forms of prayer, the Gayatri Mantra has stood out as a beacon of clarity and peace, its sacred vibrations offering resilience when I needed it most.

This book is a heartfelt collection of my thoughts and realizations, and my deepest hope is that it inspires you in some way. If you haven't yet embraced the practice of chanting the Gayatri Mantra, I encourage you to give it a try. Let its energy flow through you, bringing balance, positivity, and transformation into your life. May you experience the same peace and strength that I have found through this sacred chant. And as you weave prayer and the Gayatri Mantra into your daily life, may you also become a source of light, love, and kindness to those around you.

The Journey of Writing This Book

The inspiration behind *Echoes of the Gayatri* comes from my deep belief in the transformative power of the Gayatri Mantra. Having personally felt its positive impact, I felt a strong desire to share this sacred wisdom with others. Through this book, I hope to help more people discover the profound benefits of chanting the Gayatri Mantra and make it a part of their daily lives. I truly believe that embracing this practice can bring peace, clarity, and spiritual growth, ultimately leading to a more fulfilling life for all.

Writing this book has been a spiritual journey in itself. As I delved deeper into the meanings, practices, and experiences related to the mantra, I found myself rediscovering its power in new ways. Each word written here carries my deepest reverence and love for the mantra, and it is my sincere hope that this book serves as a small lamp, guiding you toward the greater light within you.

The Transformative Power of the Gayatri Mantra

Many people have asked me, "How does chanting a mantra bring real change?" The answer lies not only in the sound of the words but in the intention behind them. The Gayatri Mantra is a call to divine wisdom, a request to be guided toward light and knowledge. It is a prayer that aligns us with higher energies, bringing clarity where there is confusion, strength where there is weakness, and peace where there is turmoil.

I have witnessed many moments of divine grace through the Gayatri Mantra. In times of doubt, it has provided me with clarity; in times of grief, it has been a source of comfort. There have been moments when I have felt overwhelmed by life's uncertainties, and in those times, chanting the mantra has grounded me, reminding me that I am always supported by a higher force.

Bringing the Gayatri Mantra into Your Daily Life

If you are new to chanting or spiritual practices, I encourage you to start with small steps. The beauty of the Gayatri Mantra is that it does not demand elaborate rituals or conditions; it simply asks for sincerity and devotion. Here are a few ways you can incorporate it into your life:

- **Morning Meditation:** Start your day with a few repetitions of the mantra, setting a positive tone for the day.

- **Chanting Before Sleep:** Let the sacred sounds calm your mind and prepare you for restful sleep.

- **During Challenges:** When facing difficulties, silently chant the mantra to find inner strength.

- **In Moments of Gratitude:** Use the mantra as a way to express gratitude for the blessings in your life.

Even a few minutes of chanting can bring immense benefits, helping you connect with your inner self and the divine wisdom that resides within.

The Collective Power of Chanting

One of the most powerful aspects of the Gayatri Mantra is its ability to bring people together. When chanted collectively, the vibrations multiply, creating an atmosphere of peace and positivity. I have been fortunate to witness this power firsthand. There was a time when my friend's father met with a serious accident. The situation was critical, and the doctors were uncertain about the outcome. Feeling helpless yet hopeful, my friends and I gathered in our hostel and began chanting the Gayatri Mantra with all our hearts. The air was filled with devotion and prayer, and a sense of divine presence surrounded us. Miraculously, the next day, we received news that his condition had stabilized, and he had escaped major surgery. The doctors were amazed at his sudden improvement, but deep inside, we knew it was the grace of the divine that had worked through our collective prayers. This experience strengthened my faith even more and showed me that prayer, when done with pure intention, has the power to bring about real change.

The Journey Ahead

As you move forward from this book, I hope you carry with you the wisdom and peace that the Gayatri Mantra offers. Whether you chant it daily or simply reflect on its meaning from time to time, know that every small effort brings you closer to its transformative power.

Remember that spirituality is a personal journey - there is no the single right way to practice. What matters most is your sincerity and openness to experiencing the divine. The Gayatri Mantra is a gift that has been passed down for generations, and now, you have the opportunity to make it a part of your life's story.

Thank you for allowing me to share this journey with you. May the sacred vibrations of the Gayatri Mantra illuminate your path, fill your heart with peace, and guide you toward wisdom, love, and fulfillment.

Om Bhur Bhuvah Swaha...

****

Thank you for taking the time to read this book.

May the wisdom of the Gayatri Mantra bring peace,
clarity, and divine guidance into your life.